THE REGENCY COLOURING BOOK

First published in Great Britain in 2021 by
Michael O'Mara Books Limited
9 Lion Yard
Tremadoc Road
London SW4 7NQ

A CIP catalogue record for this book is available from the British Library.

Papers used by Michael O'Mara Books Limited are natural, recyclable products made from wood grown in sustainable forests. The manufacturing processes conform to the environmental regulations of the country of origin.

ISBN: 978-1- 78929-383-8 in paperback print format

1 2 3 4 5 6 7 8 9 10

Designed by Claire Cater
Written and illustrated by Amy-Jane Adams

Printed and bound in China

www.mombooks.com

MIX
Paper from responsible sources
FSC® C020056

THE REGENCY COLOURING BOOK

Michael O'Mara Books Limited

Introduction

Once upon a time in England there lived a fun and adventurous Prince named George. He loved to reveal the great wonders of the world and lived a colourful, rich, decorated existence, surrounded by eastern treasures and delights. His world became a legend and would captivate the United Kingdom, paving the way for a time forever known as 'the Regency'.

THE FEMALE TATLER BY
MRS. CRACKENTHORPE

Issue no. 41

(Friday October 7 to Monday October 10)

People that have an itch at scribbling generally entertain their visitors with their happy projects, high flights, and wonderful performances, therefore 'tis to be supposed this paper is in great measure the subject of many a drawing-room. My Lady Prudence Maxim thought 'twas exposing families too much, that now, truly, a lady could not be free and gamesome, write a Billet Doux, drink a glass of Ratafia, send her jewels out when cards run ill, or be seen in a Billet Doux, drink a glass of Hackney with her cousin the colonel, but the next morning the bawling fellow tells it to the whole town.

The major part of the world, who are the insipids, may term a paper this kind scurrilous, scandalous, and false, talk of it with an imaginable liberty, and affirm that the author has been drubbed, who perhaps can be even with those that say so. But the few wise, who are of the opinion that people are sooner ridiculed than preached out of their follies and that more may be learned out of some plays than out of some sermons, must allow, that a Tatler alarms the world into circumspection. And as pride, vanity and affectation furnish fit reproof, immorality and prophaneness are so strenuously exploded that the giddy sort gossip less for fear of being laughed at, and the libertines of the age sin more in private for fear of being abhorred.

Now though I have no plot to my play, I have a moral to may tale, which is that people of quality who squander away money upon such trifles would gain a public reputation, a private satisfaction, and set a noble example to their inferiors, in bestowing it upon the distressed Palantines, or giving it to such officers in our fleets and armies as do not think they are paid enough for making sinecures of the posts they are possessed of.

Prince George Augustus Fredrick (1762–1830) was declared as the Prince Regent in 1810, due to his father's ill-health. This is when the Regency period really began. This short-lived yet remarkable era truly flourished and manifested throughout his reign, until his death in 1830.

The Prince commissioned the architect John Nash to redesign and extend the existing Pavilion in Brighton, United Kingdom, which he named the Royal Pavilion. It was topped with enormous onion-like domes, each one filled with glistening glass panes, splashed by crashing sea waves. Snakes sculpted by master masons in golden stone climbed the outside walls and slithered over doorways. It was his ultimate pleasure palace.

Walls and furniture at the Royal Pavilion reinterpreted traditional Chinese hand-painted wallpapers, known in Europe as chinoiserie. The rich and famous had already been accustomed to decoration inspired by China but the Prince took it to a whole new level, by using it as an extraordinary theatrical backdrop. Even stained glass was adorned with chinoiserie motifs, including flowers, geometry and mythical creatures and, following soon after, so too were the clothes worn by all at the Royal Court.

Ladies at court wore dresses with gliding trains painstakingly embroidered by the leading makers in Paris and London. Made from the finest silks and trimmed in real gold and silver to shimmer along with their jewels, the new Regency style was demure and much unlike the voluminous fashions before. Light fabrics were cut streamlined with high waistlines and very short sleeves, making every female feel like a classical goddess.

When there was a party at the palace the ladies finished their ensemble with giant ostrich feathers, dyed in luminous colours, affixed in their hair and decorated with shining gems and pearls.

Dancing was energetic and performed to the sound of a live orchestra. At the Royal Pavilion, guests danced on an elaborate carpet made by Axminster, woven with twenty dragons, 100 sun rays and 274 lotus leaves. Revelers wouldn't hold back, leaping and skipping around to routines known as the 'Cotillion', a country dance, and the Scotch Reel.

The Prince Regent adored his prized Chinese pagodas. They lined the walls of the music room at the Royal Pavilion and as the people danced, so did the gold bells on each of the pagodas. The designs of these structures also featured fish, Kylin dogs and snake-entwined arrow-heads piercing winged dragons. They were made in China, comprising porcelain painted in underglaze blue, enamels and gilt, with additions in enameled pottery and mounted in gilt bronze.

The star instrument of any exclusive dancing ball or musical event was undoubtedly the Érard Harp. The Prince Regent was lucky to have his own and endorsed the craftsmanship and inventiveness of Sébastien Érard's studio. The most iconic of Érard's harp designs are the 'Angel' and 'Gothic' models, but importantly the company were pioneers in creating the modern piano as we know it, favoured by the likes of Beethoven and Chopin.

People loved to socialize and with it often came eating. The day would begin with a light breakfast of spiced cake or bread along with tea or hot chocolate. Lunch was a new affair: breakfast was being eaten earlier and dinner very late, so the stomach dictated the introduction of 'lunch', with cold meats breads and cakes being served. By night, no party or ball would be complete without a wonderful feast. If you lived by the sea like the Prince Regent, then a fish course was more than likely. Desserts and puddings were made of sponge, custard, liqueurs and fruits.

At the table, everything was served in beautifully engraved silver, with silver cutlery, too. Little pots would sit at the centre of the table, filled with condiments, sugar and jams. Sugar was considered to aid digestion and whether it was smothered over fruits or rolled with nuts, it was more than acceptable for it to cleanse the palette after every meal.

The Prince Regent was host to endless parties and feasts. In 1817 he hosted Grand Duke Nicolas of Russia in a lavish banquet at the Royal Pavilion. Antonin Carême, considered the first celebrity chef, came from Paris to prepare over 100 dishes that included a terrine of larks, rose ice-cream sundaes and an exquisitely rendered pastry sculpture of the Royal Pavilion.

Chinese-exported wallpapers brought an explosion of colour – an exotic world previously unseen in England. Excessively detailed and opulent, designers continue to find inspiration from chinoiserie today, and in particular the designs that decorated the Royal Pavilion at Brighton. One notable design created for the Pavilion was the 'Dragon' wallpaper by Robert Jones c.1820.

Ostrich feathers found their way into the bedrooms, too. The Prince Regent's bed was hung with lined silks embroidered in gold. The posts and finials were gilded to match his ornately carved mirrors and solid paneled doors. Soon after it was made, the bed had to be moved to the ground floor because the Prince was too large to make it up the stairs!

Everybody wanted a 'Kylin Clock,' as it has often incorrectly been known. Flanked by Chinese lions, or 'Dogs of Fo,' and topped with a Japanese porcelain Hotei (god of luck), elaborate mantle clocks were sought after and were displayed in a prominent position. Interestingly, these designs weren't primarily the result of craftsman based in the Far East but instead were put together in Europe using a variety of components sourced from entirely different places. This clock was displayed in the Saloon at the Royal Pavilion.

On hot, sunny days ladies put up their parasols. These must-have accessories had long handles that were often intricately carved, either out of hardwood or ivory. Parasols were made of silk or cotton and often lined in a contrasting colour to the main body and were trimmed with fringing, feathers and tassels.

The Pasha of Egypt gifted the Prince Regent a giraffe captured in the Nubian Desert. With its extraordinary long neck, nobody in England had ever seen a creature like it. The Prince's new friend travelled to England by ship along the River Nile in Africa to the island of Malta in Europe where she changed ship for one with a hole cut in the deck for her neck. Her journey to London took several weeks and from there she was taken by carriage to live in the royal garden.

THE FEMALE TATLER BY
A SOCIETY OF LADIES

Issue no. 67

(Wednesday December 7 to Friday December 9)

Emilia and I having muddled away a little of our own money, were sitting to observe the variety of the company that frequent those places, and how different their fancies were in pictures, fans, china, and such fashionable impertinences. Lady Praise-All surveyed the nick-nackatory, with an amazement, as if she had received a new sense–these cups were charming, those stones unparalleled, and such prodigious jars were never heard of–everything was displaced to oblige her ladyship's curiosity, who protested that she shouldn't grudge to spend an estate on things so prodigiously fine, drank a gallon of tea, and marched off without laying out a sixpence.

Mrs. Trifleton came so full of commissions from ladies in the country that we thought she would have emptied the warehouse and stared at the handsome 'prentice as if she expected to have him into the bargain. She wanted finer things than were ever made, and, could they have been had, would have demanded them cheaper than they were bought. She bid three half crowns for a two-guinea fan, wanted chocolate, all nut, for eighteen pence a pound, and beat down the best Imperial tea to the price of Sage o' Virtue. Japan work, she thought at an excessive rate, China images were idolatrous, India pictures were the foolishest things, she'd have had them given her a dozen. At last, having positive orders from my Lady Smoak and Sot of Exeter, to buy her a stone spitting-pot, she shook her head at the dearness of it, and ordered them to set it down to her.

Mrs. Honeysuckle was two hours pleasing herself in a paper nosegay, and Mrs. Delf employed five people to match her grout cup.

On a sudden, stops a leathern conveniency at the door, with four fellows of the world behind it, in the gayest liveries I ever saw, out of which comes a couple of quality Quakers. They moved in, like disdainful duchesses who complain of corns if they walk but cross a room, rolled about their sanctified eyes, as if it were condescension in them to appear upon earth, and with abundance of reluctancy, one of them vouchsafed us a bow, instead of a curtsy. Emilia and I were not a little pleased to remark the pride and singularity in dress, speech and behaviour in that sect of people summed up in these two statues. Their clothes were costly and without making any show, and though they abominate profane pinners and topknots, yet, by the disposition of their locks and the artful crimping of their hoods upon wires, they showed themselves equally vain, and that they had taken as much pains to be particular as other ladies do to appear like the rest of the world, yet notwithstanding all their seeming plainness, the old man had crept in among them for watches, tweezer cases, and gold chains, and a patch or two to cover pretended pimples.

When they had with secret satisfaction received all the ceremonious address of 'Ladies, your most obedient, do me the honour, etc.' which they expect from people of the world without vouchsafing any other return than a precise nod, in a sighing tone, they enquired for fine tea-tables, gilded cabinets, glass sconces, and all the richest things more proper to adorn the palace of a prince than to dizen out a yea and nay parlour in Hand Alley. Whatever bore a moderate price was trash and trumpery. 'Dost thee think my Ananias can his barley gruel out of such coarse ware?' But a Japan basin of ten guineas is fit for the pure ones to make a gooseberry fool in, and the pieces moved as gradually out of their pockets as if the spirit had directed each in its proper place, according to the seniority of their being coined.

Susanna, having drunk to much green tea, was seized with a violent fit of the colic, so that the creature Rosa Solis was forced to be called for. Rachel too, being an apprehensive of that diabolical distemper, by way of prevention, tasted of that tempting liquor, which they say, those carnal women called Duchesses guzzle. At that abominable rate, the demure sisters sipped up a whole quart, but their heads not being the least intoxicated with the pomps and the vanities of the world, it only made them cheerful, and being pure in spirit they were very much rejoiced.

But, as in this wicked age misfortunes will happen to afflict the upright, Colonel Sturdy, one of the greatest rakes that ever kept basset bank or carried doxy out of the side box, happened to reel in, seized upon Susanna, smuggled her as if she had been a beastly orange wench and swore so prodigiously that Rachel staggered, and was falling into a swoon, had not the Colonel left Susanna, and taken her into his arms. Rachel, though in wondrous confusion, had the presence of mind to say, 'Dear man, who art called Colonel, do anything to me, but don't swear.' Susanna, with robust zeal, divides Rachel and the Colonel, and told him that though he had the assurance to accost her in that lustful manner, he ought to have shown more reverence to Rachel, who had been a speaker these seven years. Rachel accused Susanna of incivility, and said, 'What the man did to thee, sister, was blame worthy, and though ought'st to chide him for't, but 'twas kind and tender in him to support my weakness, or I had stumbled and fell.'

In short, the sanctified sisters quarrelled so about a libertine, whom even loose women that sin with some restraint abominate for his inconstancy, that 'twas with no small struggling they concealed their enmity from the servants and went home together in the same coach. Emlia and I were so crowded with reflections on what we had seen, that we had hardly patience to vent them without interrupting each other, but at length our sentiments appeared to be much the same, that Quakers are the most designing, deceitful sect of creatures in the world, who assume more pride and exact more homage from their seeming sanctity, than the truly pious, who are always easy and unconstrained.

Their houses are as richly and gaily furnished as those of quality, their equipages as glaring, and though they affect a ridiculous habit, a primness of air, and screw themselves up like trussed rabbits, yet they are as foppish their way, and by little and little wink at one another in those modes and fancies, which they term Babylonish, idolatrous, and diabolical. They love music and dancing, though they won't practice it themselves, read play though they won't see them, will sneak into a tavern at the back door, fornicate with a Holy Sister, and if, by subtlety in trade, they can over-reach their neighbours, 'tis but engrossing to themselves the spoils of the wicked. The young Quakers of both sexes are so far gone from truth, as to arrive at most libertines of the age. The men play as high at Roly-Poly and the women coquet as much upon the walks, and 'tis no novelty nowadays to see, a Fleet Street Sylvia whip into a tavern with a Damon that had no button holes behind.

Horses were the primary mode of transport and a necessity in Regency England, especially if you lived in the city during the week and spent your weekends in the country. The Prince Regent commissioned the architect John Nash to design new stables at Buckingham Palace. The accommodation for his four-legged friends was state-of-the-art, built on a central quadrangle and entered via a dramatic classical Doric-style arch. A principle coach house contained his father King George III's iconic Gold State Coach.

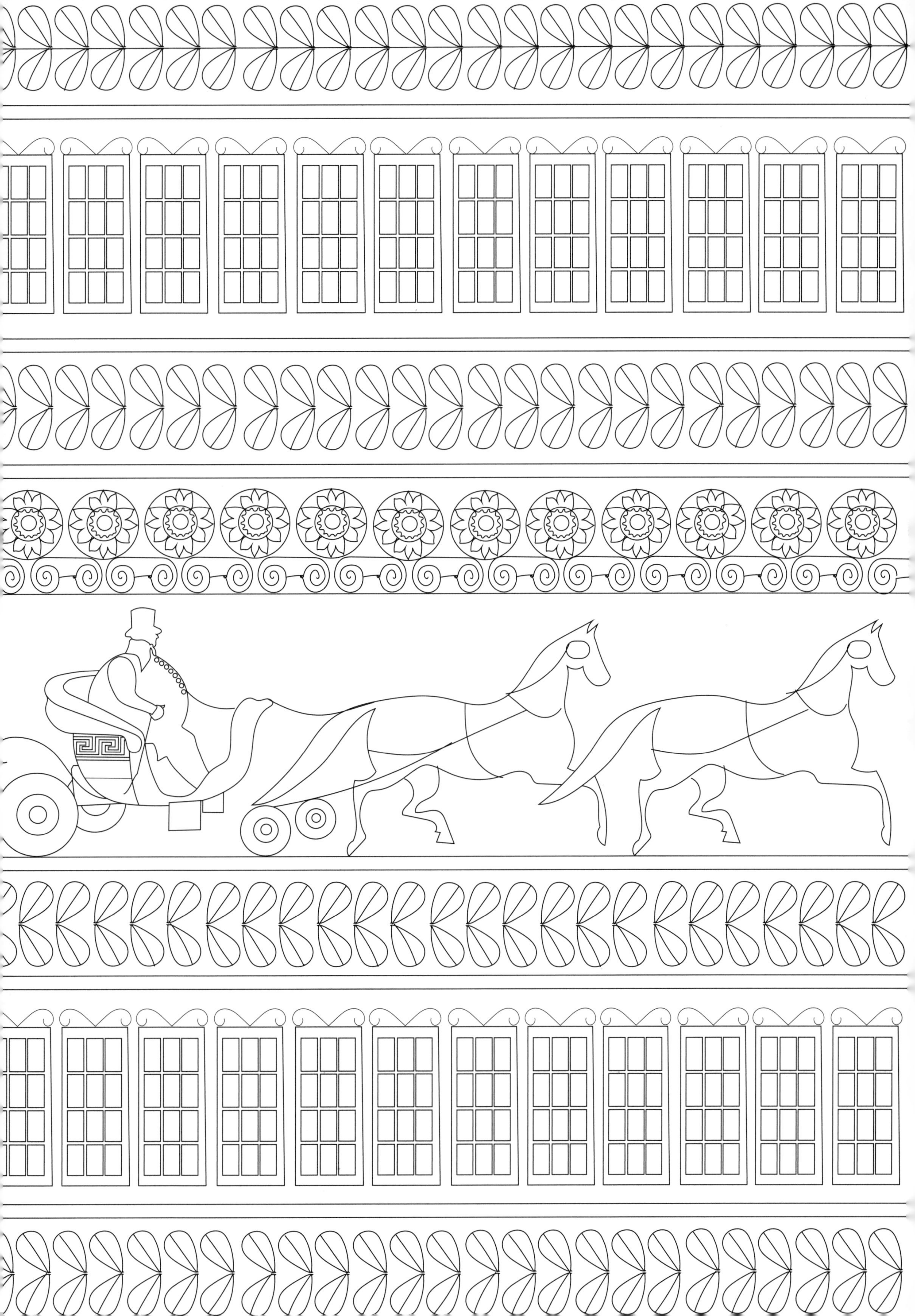

Elegant townhouses standing several storeys high lined England's town and city streets, the walls decorated in patterned stucco and glazed with vast windows designed to take in the light. The Regency townhouse was based on an already familiar design that consisted of domestic offices for servants in the basement, formal rooms for entertaining on the ground and first floors and bedrooms above. Behind the townhouse would be a small mews with a coach house, stables and a small home for the coachman and grooms.

Coaches were designed to be pulled by horses. They could accommodate several people and were as varied in style as today's cars. The nobility preferred to make theirs bespoke and paint their coat of arms on the outside. The inside was upholstered in horse hair and leather for comfort. However, roads were very rough due to the ever-changing English weather, so travelling long distances by coach could be uncomfortable – and by night the threat of highwaymen made journeys more dangerous than adventurous.

If you loved horsepower in Regency England you'd probably own a 'curricle' – a vehicle meant for two horses. Small and with only two wheels, curricles had a hood that folded down, similar to today's convertible cars. Lightweight and very fast, it was a favourite of young men – including the Prince Regent – who liked to go faster. The curricle was used in racing, but with its lightweight body tipped over easily, giving it the risk factor sought by any thrill seeker.

The streets of London, Brighton and Bath were filled with beautiful ornate iron railings inspired by designs from India and the Far East. Much of it was still handmade by blacksmiths – known as 'wrought' iron – but it was thanks to the development of cast iron that decorative pieces soon appeared on street corners, in parks and even seating.

For the Regency lady a shopping trip was quite a treat. The interiors of each shop were beautifully decorated, with gilded and carved Corinthian capitals, glass skylights and grand staircases. A gallery space allowed art to be displayed so shopping could be made an enriching experience. The shopping arcades consisted of several stalls and wholesale warehouses selling clothes, jewellery and furs. The most popular was undoubtedly London's Western Exchange, also known as the 'Bond Street Bazaar'.

The very first department store was Harding, Howell & Co. Situated on London's Pall Mall, it was designed in the classical style, made up of four departments that included furs and fans, haberdashery selling silks, muslin, gloves and lace, and suppliers of French clocks and porcelain from the Far East.

Shoes were delicate and made of silk, velvet and satins. They were hand embroidered with beautiful flowers and tightened with a drawstring. The finest shoes were produced by maker George Hoby, whose boots were worn by four royal dukes – Kent, Cumberland, Sussex and Cambridge. Large quantities of women's shoes were also imported from France.

Dresses were brightly coloured and layered with fine, dream-like netting, known as 'tulle', that was richly embroidered with flowers. The shape that encapsulates the era featured a high waist, low neckline and small puff sleeves. White muslin was worn during the day and silks were reserved for the evening.

A century before the East India Company imported Indian paisley fabrics, Indian-inspired paisley surface patterns for cotton and woven cashmere became evermore popular, with their bright colours and bold exotic botanical motifs such as palm, cypress and pine trees. Paisleys were printed in France but also in Scotland in the town from which it takes its name.

Paisley shawls were a wardrobe staple for any Regency woman and they began to be mass produced to meet demand. To speed up the manufacturing process and make the fashion item more affordable block printing was used. Paisley is also referred to as 'The Persian Pickle' (America) or 'Welsh Pears' (Wales).

Vast collections of inspirational and intriguing artefacts had been gathered by aristocrats on a grand tour for over a century and this passion grew with a new surge of wealthy but curious manufacturers and successful entrepreneurs in England. As a result of their fascination, they amassed collections that were soon exhibited. One man in particular was William Bullock, who commissioned the Egyptian Hall in Piccadilly, London, to display items from the South Seas, brought back to England by Captain Cook. It was the first building in England inspired by the Egyptian style.

MUSEUM

The Egyptian Hall was designed by Peter Fredrick Robinson, a former employee of architect Henry Holland. It had an iconic façade inspired by the drawings of Egypt by the French artist, author and diplomat Dominique Vivant, Baron Denon, who is considered the father of modern Egyptology.

The legendary home of Thomas Hope that inspired the hall stood just a short walk from the museum itself. Hope was an artist, designer and collector who, like William Bullock, had vast wealth that he used to invest in ancient artefacts and sculptures. Hope's greatest legacy is undoubtedly his designs for furniture – he created striking seating inspired by Egypt for his grand London home. His reputation as one of England's greatest designers was established in his book *Household Furniture and Interior Decoration*.

Just like the Prince Regent, Thomas Hope was inspired by the world, decorating rooms according to the countries he'd visited. Famously, his collection of Greek and southern Italian vases was so vast they were exhibited across three rooms. Hope opened the doors to his collection and and made his home a house-museum.

At the Egyptian Hall, exhibitions comprised of Bullock's 32,000 objects of ethnological, archaeological and natural history. With his permanent collection growing in popularity, Bullock began to hold temporary exhibitions, the most famous of which was 'Modern Mexico', in which visitors meandered through a jungle of prickly pears overshadowed by stone-carved serpents.

William Bullock acquired the artefacts for his 1824 exhibition during a visit to Mexico a year before. Major archaeological excavations had been undertaken in Mexico City at the end of the eighteenth century and significant finds could be acquired, including the Aztec calendar 'sun stone' a three-and-a-half-metre (11.8 feet) basalt relief of the Mexica creation myth.

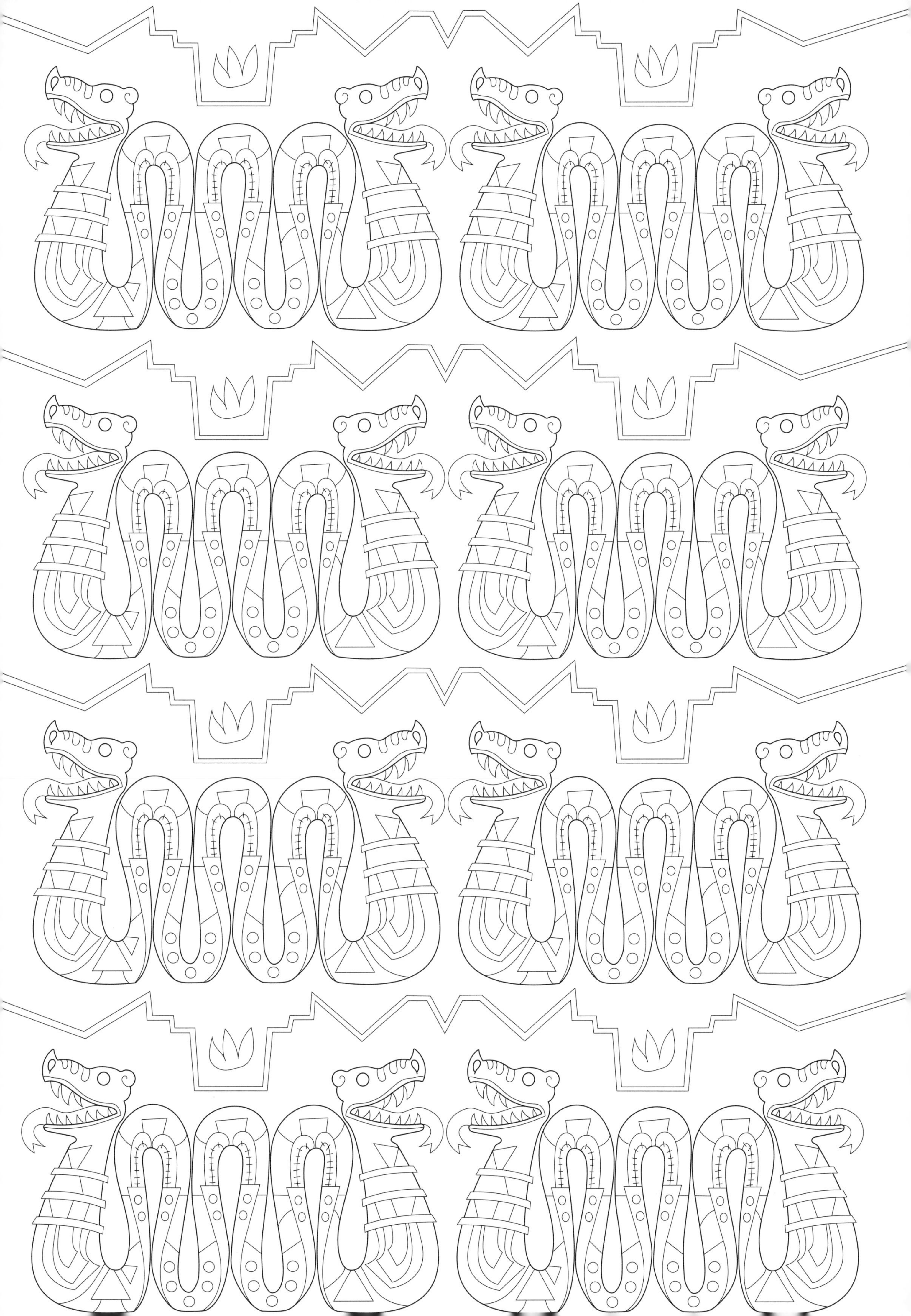

Before the Prince Regent's lifetime, streets were unlit at night. First there was the oil lamp, but they were costly and something only the rich could afford. However, soon came the introduction of gas lighting, In London an experimental scheme to light Pall Mall was completed in 1807.

In and around London's most exclusive addresses, including private members' club White's, you'd find a 'dandy' – an incredibly well dressed, flamboyant, quick-witted soul – rubbing shoulders with an aristocrat. The most famous of these was a man named George 'Beau' Brummell.

For entertainment, people headed to London's Vauxhall Gardens, a pleasure garden situated on the south side of the river Thames. Already well established, it was landscaped with avenues of trees and buildings including a Chinese Pavilion, rotunda and Turkish tent ...

… Contemporary music from the most notable composers and musicians of the day performed on an octagonal orchestra stand. This stage promoted the latest in English music.

Aside from the classical arts there were awe-inspiring circus acts and acrobatics. The gardens soon became a place for fun as well as relaxation with tightrope walkers and trapeze artists.

'Vauxhall Gardens is peculiarly adapted to the taste of the English nation; there being a mixture of curious show, — gay exhibition, musick, vocal and instrumental, not too refined for the general ear; — for all of which only a shilling is paid; and, though last, not least, good eating and drinking for those who choose to purchase that regale.'

James Boswell

Endless avenues and walkways were lit by thousands of lights at night, while darker corners provided another secret world. Londoners of all classes and ranks would enjoy the space together.

Hot air balloon rides were the most exciting spectacle, and many were launched from Vauxhall Gardens. As a young man, the Prince Regent witnessed the first hot air balloon flight navigated by Italian Vincenzo Lunardi above London.

Regency Lords and Ladies loved fireworks and at the Vauxhall Gardens they watched incredible displays in orange and white delivered by talented 'fire masters.'

Fireworks sparked brightly in the London sky and brightened every rooftop. A short distance from Vauxhall Gardens stood the Prince Regent's favourite London residence, Carlton House.

Architect Henry Holland was commissioned to design the Prince's neoclassical Carlton House. The interior was a dramatic mix of gothic and classical design, with fan-vaulted ceilings inspired by English cathedrals. Later, with the help of John Nash, the mansion linked fashionable St James' with The Regent's Park.

The mansion was filled with gothic and classical treasures including velvet upholstered seating known as the Roman council chairs. They were designed and made by Marsh & Tatham (subsequently Tatham, Bailey & Sanders).

The most affordable Regency wallpapers for interiors were often striped and block printed by hand. Chinese papers were imported and featured non-repeating pictorial scenes – these were a real luxury and extremely costly to import.

On the first floor of the Royal Pavilion the walls were covered in beautiful hand-painted chinoiserie paper. This was subsequently moved by Queen Victoria to Buckingham Palace and then parts of it returned to the Pavilion in the 1920s. The design features magnolia trees, hanging baskets and peonies.

The White Hart and Red Lion have always been the most popular pub names in England. During the Regency era some pubs were renamed The Prince Regent in honour of the Prince.

THE
PRINCE
REGENT

John Nash is the principle architect who defined the era's buildings. He was commissioned by the Prince Regent to rebuild a large part of London known as The Regent's Park. The area consisted of landscaped gardens, water fountains, grand crescents, villas and London Zoo.

London Zoo was first established strictly for scientific study and not for public viewing. At the time of the Prince Regent's death, it became the new home for all the animals who lived at the Tower of London's royal menagerie.

Unlike the cities, the countryside changed little and architecturally remained the same as it had been for several hundreds of years. Life in the country was led purely by the seasons, agriculture and farming. Illumination was still by candlelight and the church bells chimed the hours.

Great tithe barns stored crops for livestock, and straw for building walls. And the cockerel called and woke everyone at sunrise ...

Jane Austen lived in Bath with her parents for several years. She set two novels in the city – *Northanger Abbey* and *Persuasion*. Bath was considered the place to be favoured by royalty and celebrities of the day, who retreated there for the perfect balance of work and play. The city had everything London had to offer. Austen would have been well connected, enjoying a very busy social life and mixing in both artistic and academic circles.

4
4

The Prince Regent admired Jane Austen's novels and owned a set for each of his homes. In 1815, the royal librarian invited Austen to visit the Prince in London and expressed a wish that she dedicate her latest novel, *Emma,* to him. Due to his womanizing and wild lifestyle, the author wasn't a fan of the Prince and was irritated by his librarian's tiresome title suggestions.

NORTHANGER ABBEY:

AND

PERSUASION.

BY THE AUTHOR OF "PRIDE AND PREJUDICE,"
"MANSFIELD-PARK," &c.

WITH A BIOGRAPHICAL NOTICE OF THE
AUTHOR

IN FOUR VOLUMES

VOL. 1.

LONDON :
JOHN MURRAY, ALBERMARLE-STREET.

1818

In 1820 the Prince Regent's father King George III died and he was crowned King at Westminster Abbey, London, on 19 July 1821. The Prince, true to his style, made sure the ceremony was the most lavish in history: participants were requested to wear Tudor- and Stuart-style costumes. The Prince wore a lavishly embroidered twenty-seven-foot (8.2 metres) red velvet robe with a long train and, due to its weight, is said to have had the most uncomfortable day of his life.

GR O IV
hall
no. 265

ABOUT THE ILLUSTRATOR

Amy Jane Adams (AJ) is a British author, painter, installation artist, illustrator, photographer and set designer. She is particularly obsessed with buildings and the people who lived in them and is inspired by the Italian Renaissance, pop art and graffiti. Her clients include Jenny Packham, National Trust, Royal Institute of British Architects (RIBA) and Church of England. She has exhibited at the Courtauld Institute of Art (2010) and Gloucester Cathedral (2017) who became host to a 30-metre length 'carpet' designed by the artist and painted by over 1,000 visitors to the world-famous heritage site. She lives and works in London.